HIGHES
AND
LOWEST

Harcourt
SCHOOL PUBLISHERS

Visit *The Learning Site!* www.harcourtschool.com

Highest and Lowest Places on Earth

People climb this mountain.

Mount Everest

Nothing lives in this sea.

The Dead Sea

Hottest and Coldest Places on Earth

In summer, it is hot here.

Death Valley, California

Few animals live in this cold place.

Antarctica

Wettest and Driest Places on Earth

Heavy rains fall here.

Cherrapungi, India

This land gets no rain.

The Atacama Desert

Think and Respond

1. What is the highest place on Earth?

2. Why can few animals live in Antarctica?

3. Which place would you like to visit? Why?

Activity

With a partner, act out being in one of the places in the book.